HOW THEY LIVED

A TUDOR MERCHANT

BARRY AND ANNE STEEL

Illustrated by
John James

HOW THEY LIVED

First published in 1986 by
Wayland (Publishers) Limited
61 Western Road, Hove
East Sussex BN3 1JD, England

© Copyright 1986 Wayland (Publishers) Limited

British Library Cataloguing in Publication Data
Steel, Barry
A Tudor Merchant. — (How they lived)
1. England — Social life and customs — 16th
century — Juvenile literature
I. Title II. Steel, Anne III. James, John, 1959-
IV. Series
942.05'5   DA356

ISBN 0-85078-547-2

Typeset by Planagraphic Typesetters Limited
Printed and bound in Belgium by
Casterman S.A.

CONTENTS

MERCHANT ADVENTURERS

On the busy London dockside a group of well-dressed merchants watched excitedly as a large-masted wooden ship edged slowly up to its mooring. Soon they were aboard, eagerly inspecting its cargo of brightly-coloured silks, cotton, olive oil, currants and spices. Each of the merchants owned a share in the cargo, and they expected it to fetch at least £70,000.

They smiled with satisfaction. It was a fine return for the cheap cargo of cloth, tin, pewter and rabbit skins they had sent to the Mediterranean in the same ship six weeks earlier.

The year was 1595. Elizabeth I, last of the Tudor monarchs, was Queen of England. It was a time of adventure and excitement. English sailors were trading in Africa, the Far East and

The ships of the Spanish Armada were defeated by the English fleet.

America. Fifteen years earlier, Sir Francis Drake had sailed round the world, and seven years before he had helped defeat the great Spanish Armada. England was fighting and winning a sea war against Spain but there was peace at home. It was a great age for English music, poetry and theatre — at that time a young playwright called William Shakespeare was becoming famous. It was also a great age for scientific discovery. Most people were better off than they had ever been. Some could even afford expensive foreign luxuries, so the merchants would have no trouble selling their cargo.

TUDOR SOCIETY

The most important people in Tudor England, after the Royal Family, were the nobles — the earls, lords and barons from whom the Queen usually chose her courtiers and ministers. Almost as important were the rich country landowners known as the gentry. They too could hold positions at the Queen's court and in government.

Merchants were often richer than nobles or gentlemen, but they did not hold such a high place in society. This was because, unlike nobles and the gentry, who had inherited the wealth of their ancestors, merchants had made their fortunes by their own work. They belonged to the same social group as people like lawyers and wealthy farmers. They were far richer and more important than ordinary people, especially in the towns.

Associations of merchants called livery companies or guilds controlled the town and city councils, and mayors and aldermen were often merchants. As the population grew, and as more people wanted goods from distant countries, merchants became more and more important.

Below the merchant class came skilled craftsmen like tailors, bakers and goldsmiths, who ran their own small businesses. Lower down still came the biggest group, the wage earners, who worked for other people. Finally came the unemployed and the beggars, who often turned to crime.

A merchant of modest income.

A pyramid diagram, showing the different levels of Tudor society.

Royalty

Noblemen

Wealthy merchants,
landowners
and lawyers

Skilled craftsmen
and traders

Peasants
and beggars

7

A MERCHANT'S WORK

Merchants earned their living by trade. The richest of them traded with other countries. These are the merchants you can read about in this book. They bought goods from the makers in England and shipped them to foreign countries, where they traded them for other goods. When the foreign goods were brought back to England, the merchants sold them to shopkeepers and traders, who then sold them to the public. Merchants made their money, of course, by buying goods cheaply and selling them at a higher price. Some merchants traded mainly in one type of goods, but most were happy to make their profits buying and selling whatever they could.

Much of a merchant's long working day was spent arguing with suppliers

London's Royal Exchange was the centre of merchant trade.

A merchant working in his warehouse.

and customers about prices and delivery dates, perhaps at the Royal Exchange in London. This was the city's main meeting place for merchants. At other times he would travel to different towns, jolting along bumpy tracks in stage-coaches. There would also be visits to his warehouse, to see that his goods were being properly guarded against thieves. Sometimes he would need to meet ship owners, to charter a ship for his next cargo. He might even travel abroad to meet his suppliers. Best of all would be the meetings with his book-keepers in his counting house, where he could add up his profits.

TRADE

In Tudor times, England's main export was a rough, unfinished woollen material known as white cloth. The only merchants allowed to trade in this were the Merchant Adventurers Company of London. In the early sixteenth century, the cloth was shipped from London to Antwerp in Belgium. After about 1575 it was sent to other ports, especially Hamburg and Emden in North Germany and Middelburg in the Netherlands.

A map of Tudor trade routes.

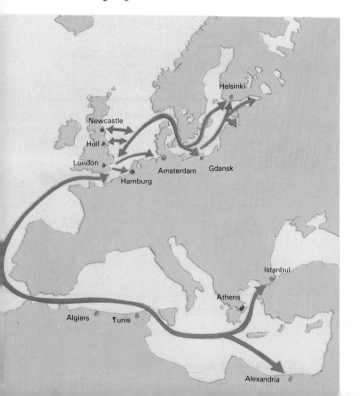

There it was sold to merchants who sent it all over Europe to be dyed, finished and re-sold.

During Queen Elizabeth's reign, several important companies of merchants were founded, to open other trade routes. In 1555 the Muscovy Company was set up to export such goods as cloth, tin, paper and wine to Russia, in exchange for rope, whale oil, tallow (animal fat used for candle making) and sealskin. The Eastland Company exported dyed, finished cloth from London, Ipswich, Hull and Newcastle to countries round the Baltic sea — Poland, Sweden, Finland and Russia. The return cargoes from the Baltic included salt, timber, tar for shipbuilding, hemp for rope making and nitre for gunpowder. Trade with the area we would now call the Middle East was controlled by the Levant Company, which traded English cloth, tin, pewter and rabbit skins in exchange for currants, silk, cotton, soap, olive oil and spices.

Right *A Middle-Eastern port.*

NEW WORLDS

In the reign of Queen Elizabeth I, English merchants began to look beyond Europe. In 1562 a group of London merchants fitted out a ship for John Hawkins, who sailed from Plymouth to Guinea in West Africa. There he traded his cargo of pots, pans, knives, beads and other cheap items for black slaves. He then sailed to the Caribbean, and exchanged his slaves for a valuable cargo of silver, pearls, rum, sugar and ginger. Hawkins sailed again in 1564 and in 1567. This third voyage ended in disaster. All but one of his ships were lost after an attack by the Spaniards at San Juan de Ulua in Mexico.

A map of routes opened by Drake, Hawkins, Frobisher and Davis.

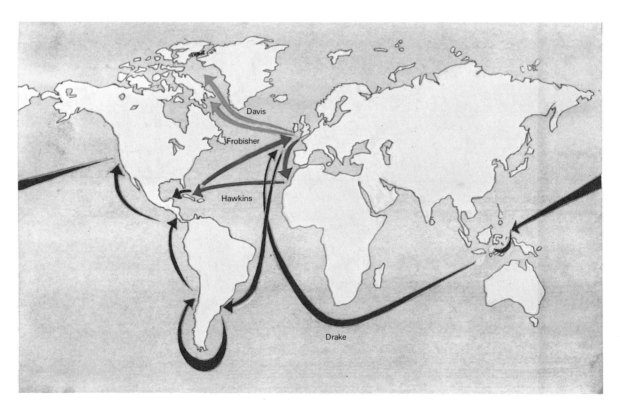

In 1577 Sir Francis Drake made his famous voyage round the world in the *Golden Hind,* returning with thirty tonnes of silver bar, diamonds and rubies, and ten tonnes of ginger, pepper and nutmegs. Drake's voyages had more to do with war than with trade, but part of the money for them was provided by respectable merchants.

Merchants also provided the money

While sailing near Greenland, Frobisher was attacked by Eskimos.

for, first, Martin Frobisher and, later, John Davis, to search for a way to the Far East round the north coast of Canada — the famous North West Passage. Unfortunately no such passage exists. Merchants also helped fund Sir Walter Raleigh's unsuccessful efforts to start a colony in America. 13

SEAPORTS

By far the biggest port in Tudor times was London. Other east coast ports, such as Ipswich, Hull and Newcastle were also very busy. The West Country ports of Bristol, Plymouth, Dartmouth and Exeter became more important as trade with America and Africa developed.

Tudor seaports would seem very small to us, but they were busy and exciting places. Among the crowds in the narrow streets there were porters pushing barrows or carrying baskets, sailors talking in strange foreign languages and perhaps a street entertainer with his performing bear. Wooden carts, piled high with bales of cloth, sacks of sugar or barrels of wine, rumbled along on the unpaved streets.

The tall buildings — houses, shops and workshops — were crammed together, sometimes with brightly painted wooden signs creaking and swaying over the doors. Traders advertised their wares from their shop

doorways or market stalls with cries of 'Ripe cowcumbers ripe!', 'Apples fine!' and 'What do ye lack?'.

Near the docks were the warehouses and counting houses of the merchants, and the customs house where they paid duty on their cargoes. Here too were the ships' chandlers who sold rope, tar, sailcloth, lanterns and other supplies. There were also inns crowded with rough looking sailors. On the quayside itself, sweating dockers hurried up and down narrow gangplanks, carrying sacks and barrels on and off ships. Carpenters, caulkers and sailmakers worked feverishly to prepare ships for their next voyage.

Above *The coat of arms of Bristol, a major Tudor Port.*

Below *A busy Tudor quayside.*

A MERCHANT SHIP

Merchant ships were usually about 25-30 m (85-95 ft) long and made of wood. Most ships had three masts. The main mast and the fore mast each carried two 'square rigged' canvas sails set across the ship's decks. The stern (or mizzen) mast had a triangular 'lateen' sail, set 'fore and aft' along the decks.

We can be less sure about the design of the inside of the hull. The picture opposite shows a large merchant ship of late Tudor times. Near the bow of the ship was a raised deck called the forecastle, below which the cook room was often situated. At the stern was a second, raised deck called the quarter-deck. On some larger merchant ships, like the one illustrated, a poop-deck was situated above the quarter-deck. Below the poop-deck was the captain's cabin, while cabins for the ship's officers were situated below the quarter-deck. Here too the helmsman steered the ship with a vertical lever called the whipstaff. This was attached to the tiller on the deck below. The carpenter, sailmaker, cooper (barrel-maker) and other ship's craftsmen worked here. Because of the danger from pirates, merchant ships usually carried a few light cannon. Later ships sometimes had a special gun deck.

The lowest part of the ship was the ship's stores, where the cargo was kept, along with the anchor chains, food, water, gunpowder and other supplies.

Left *Ships like this one sailed to many distant lands, returning with precious cargoes.*

Right *A cut-away view of a grand Tudor merchant ship.*

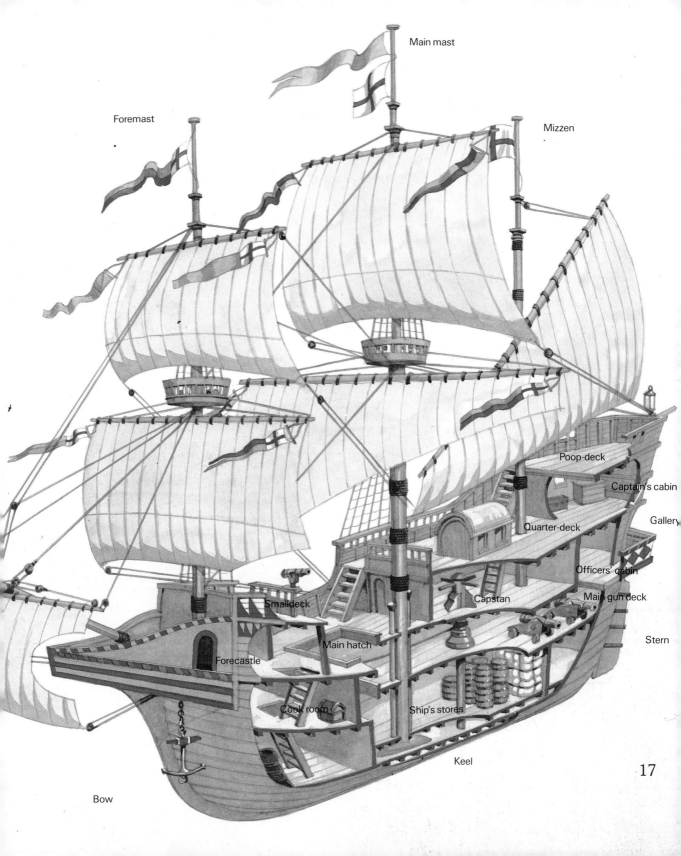

Main mast

Foremast

Mizzen

Poop-deck

Captain's cabin

Gallery

Quarter-deck

Officers' cabin

Main gun deck

Capstan

Stern

Smalldeck

Main hatch

Forecastle

Cook room

Ship's stores

Keel

Bow

17

SAILORS

Tudor merchant ships usually carried between forty and one hundred officers and crew. The master was in charge of everyone and everything on board, and his most important job was navigating the ship by the sun, stars and compass. His second-in-command was called the mate. The ship also carried skilled craftsmen like the carpenter, sail maker and barrel maker (cooper).

The ordinary crew men were very tough. They came from the poorest families. They were often men who could not find jobs ashore, or even criminals escaping from the law. They did all the hard, dangerous and dirty jobs, like carrying stores, climbing the rigging and cleaning out the bilge. They slept on the crowded decks wherever they could find a space — hammocks were not used at this time.

A seaman's food was salt pork, fish and beef, ship's biscuit, and dried yellow peas. He was allowed a gallon of beer a day to drink. Often the meat was rotten, the biscuits crawling with maggots and the beer stale. When food ran short, he might have to eat penguins, sea lions or even the rats which ran all over the ship.

In these conditions diseases like food poisoning, malaria, yellow fever and, worst of all, scurvy were common. Sometimes half the crew might die on a voyage, so extra men were always carried on board.

Above *Some items used by a Tudor sailor, including a rosary, a whistle and a pocket sundial.*

Right *Life on deck was always busy for the sailors.*

18

A FINE HOUSE

Most Tudor merchants lived in large town houses with timber frames, usually made of oak. The spaces between the timbers were filled with wattle and plaster. Only the very rich lived in brick or stone houses. Tudor towns were very crowded and many people would live under the same roof. Some houses would have four or five storeys, with each jutting out further than the one below. This was called oversailing. Glass was very expensive, but some merchants could afford large windows, which made the rooms lighter and more pleasant.

The furniture was usually of oak and included heavy, straight-backed

These items of furniture once belonged to a Tudor merchant.

chairs, stools, benches, large tables and carved storage chests. Only the very rich bought furniture with padded seats and soft coverings. Merchants slept in massive four-poster beds with heavy curtains to keep out draughts. They had feather mattresses and pillows. The floors were usually covered with rush mats. Carpets were thought much too precious to walk on, so people hung them on the walls beside their tapestries for warmth and decoration. Sometimes walls had oak panelling

A fine four-poster bed from a prosperous Tudor merchant's house in Tenby, Wales.

called wainscoting. This too made the rooms look and feel warmer.

Merchants' houses contained large fireplaces with a wood or coal fire. Because of the unpleasant smell from coal, chimneys were gradually built taller, so that the smoke would drift above the town. Lighting was provided by candles or rushes which had been soaked in fat. 21

FAMILY LIFE

Each busy day began soon after dawn with family prayers, and ended at around 9.00 pm, often with evening prayers. People had more children than nowadays, and they usually shared their home with sick or aged relatives. Parents were very strict and thought beating was good for children. Boys and girls had to kneel in front of their father to ask forgiveness or to ask a favour. Boys over seven went to school between 6.00 am and 5.30 pm, returning home for about an hour at lunchtime. Girls usually stayed at home and were taught to read and write by their parents, older brothers, or governesses. Merchants' daughters needed to learn to write letters and

In Tudor times, girls stayed at home to learn to read.

Only the boys went to school, where the teachers kept strict discipline.

keep accounts. They also learned how to run a home. Girls usually married between the ages of fourteen and sixteen, and boys at about eighteen. They often lived in their parents' home after marriage.

A fairly wealthy merchant employed men and maid servants. His wife had to organize them, and make sure that everything was done properly — cleaning, washing, mending, shopping at the local market and growing herbs in the garden for cooking and medicines. She also had to keep a caring eye on the apprentices, who lived with the merchant's family for seven years while learning the trade. They were often treated more like sons than workers.

FOOD AND DRINK

In a Tudor merchant's household there were three meals a day. Breakfast might consist of fresh bread, butter, honey and a little cold ham, with ale to drink. Supper, at around 6.00 pm, was only a little heavier than breakfast. The main meal was at mid-day, when people often ate large amounts of meat, usually roasted on a spit. Beef, venison, mutton, veal, pheasant and chicken were all popular. For a change people ate roasted larks and blackbirds — sometimes these were baked in a pie!

In winter time, when there was no fresh meat, dried and salted meat was eaten. Often it was badly kept, and to take away the unpleasant taste, it was cooked with honey, herbs, spices and rich sauces. Few vegetables were eaten, as people did not think they had much food value. The potato had been brought back from America, but it was not yet very popular. The Tudors loved sweet foods such as crystallised fruits, tarts, cakes and jellies. They were known for their very bad teeth! Ale and wine were drunk with all meals, as water and milk were not safe to drink. Children drank a lighter brew of ale.

Merchants used plates and cups made of pewter and silver. The very rich might drink from glasses. Meals were eaten with steel knives, spoons and fingers. Forks were not used at this time. Bowls of water were kept handy at mealtimes for washing greasy fingers.

Left *A pewter flagon, spoons and wooden bowls used in Tudor times.*

Right *A family mealtime.*

FASHIONS

A merchant trading in the 1590s usually wore a linen shirt, a close-fitting woollen doublet, short padded breeches and long woollen stockings called hose. He might have small ruffs at his wrist or neck. He wore leather shoes or knee-length leather boots. His cloak was short, often braided or embroidered round the edge. Older men might wear a long cloak edged with fur. Men of all classes wore beards, usually short pointed ones.

No matter how rich a merchant might be, he was not allowed to dress like the nobles and gentry, with their gorgeous materials, showy fashions, huge neck ruffs, rich embroidery and jewellery. Special laws called 'sumptuary laws' laid down rules about the kind of clothes people could wear. One law forbade merchants to wear jewelled swords like the ones worn by nobles and gentry. A few merchants ignored the laws and paid heavy fines if they were caught.

Merchants' wives wore plain, dark coloured dresses, often with detachable sleeves and padded shoulder wings. They might be decorated with braid round the hem and have small ruffs at the neck or wrist. Very rich merchants' wives might wear fur trimmings and gold ornaments. Their hair was usually tied up under a small cap.

Both boys and girls under six years old wore ankle length dresses. After the age of six, they were dressed like their parents.

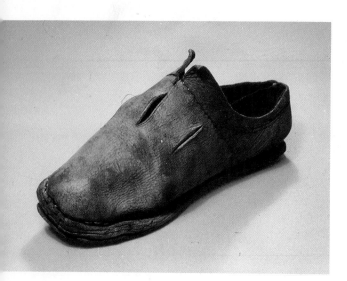

Left *A man's leather shoe from Tudor times.*

Right *A merchant and his family, wearing typical Tudor costumes.*

27

RECREATION AND RELIGION

A favourite pastime in Tudor times was watching plays. These were acted out on the back of a cart in the street or in the courtyard of an inn, but by the 1590s theatres were being built. The most famous was the Globe in London, where Shakespeare worked. It was circular, with a stage jutting out into a round space called the pit, which was open to the sky. People called the 'groundlings' only paid a penny to watch from the pit. Covered seats around the sides cost about a shilling (5p) and merchants would have used these. All the performers at this time were men or boys, and they acted without scenery or curtains.

The Tudors loved music. They sang and played instruments like the lute, viol and an early keyboard instrument, the virginal. Bull-baiting, bear-baiting and cock-fighting were other entertainments popular mainly with poorer people.

Religion was an important part of life for everyone in Tudor England. In 1559 Queen Elizabeth I had abolished the Catholic Church and set up the Church of England. New laws forced everyone to attend their local church on Sundays and holy days. Those who did not go were heavily fined. The services in the new Church of England were in English, not in Latin as the old Roman Catholic services had been.

Some people still carried on their Catholic faith, holding services in secret in their homes. In some houses secret places called 'priest holes' were built to hide Catholic priests. Some of these priest holes still remain today in houses from this period.

Left *A selection of Tudor musical instruments.*

Right *A play in progress at the Globe Theatre.*

THE END OF THE TUDORS

On 24 March 1603, Elizabeth I died peacefully. This was the end of the Tudor family. But it was certainly not the end of the growth in British trade, exploration and power at sea which had made such a promising beginning in the Tudor age. Much of the credit for this beginning belongs to the Tudor merchants. Because of their need to find new trade routes, they provided much of the money and encouragement for English sailors to develop their skills on the high seas — skills which later made Britain the world's leading sea power. It was merchants, too, who formed the East India company to trade with India. This was the first step in the growth of the vast Empire which Britain ruled at the death of Queen Victoria nearly 300 years later.

After Tudor times, merchant ships ventured to many other countries.

GLOSSARY

Bilge The very bottom, curved part of a ship's hull.

Caulker A workman who repaired holes in a ship's hull.

Charter To hire a vehicle.

Doublet A close-fitting jacket worn by men in Tudor times.

Elizabeth I The daughter of King Henry VIII and Anne Boleyn born in 1533. She was Queen of England from 1558 to 1603.

Hemp A plant used to make rope.

Livery Company A society of merchants belonging to a particular trade. Each Company had its own uniform, or livery.

Pewter A silver-grey metal made by mixing tin and lead.

Scurvy A disease common in sailors in the past.

Spanish Armada The great fleet of ships sent by Philip II of Spain against England in 1558.

Tapestry Heavy cloth with a picture or pattern woven into it.

Tiller The lever attached to a ship's rudder, used in the steering system.

Tudors A line of English royalty ruling from 1485 to 1603.

Wattle Woven twigs which were covered in plaster, and used to make the walls of houses.

MORE BOOKS TO READ

Leonard Cowie, *The Age of Drake* (Wayland, 1972)

Paul Fincham, *Tudor Town and Court Life* (Longman, 1968)

Peggy Miller, *Life in Elizabethan London* (Methuen, 1976)

Ann Mitchell, *The Tudor Family* (Wayland, 1972)

Avis Murton Carter, *One Day in Shakespeare's England* (Tyndall, 1973)

Tim Pashley, *The Tudors* (Wayland, 1985)

Stephen White-Thomson, *Elizabeth I and Tudor England* (Wayland, 1984)

INDEX

Picture acknowledgements
The pictures in this book were supplied by the following: Mary Evans Picture Library 8; The Mary Rose Trust 18, 24, 26, 28; By courtesy of the National Maritime Museum 5; The National Trust/Erik Pelham 20, 21. The remaining pictures belong to the Wayland Picture Library.